Creative Kitchen Crafts

Kathy Ross

illustrated by
Nicole in den Bosch

M Millbrook Press/Minneapolis

For Julianna and Ashlyn
—KR

Millbrook Press
A division of Lerner Publishing Group, Inc.
241 First Avenue North
Minneapolis, MN 55401 U.S.A.

Website address: www.lernerbooks.com

Library of Congress Cataloging-in-Publication Data

Ross, Kathy (Katharine Reynolds), 1948–
    Creative kitchen crafts / by Kathy Ross ; illustrated by Nicole in den Bosch.
       p.   cm. — (Girl crafts)
    ISBN: 978–0–8225–9217–4 (lib. bdg. : alk. paper)
    1. Handicraft for girls—Juvenile literature. I. Bosch, Nicole in den. II. Title.
TT171.R6823 2011
745.5—dc22   2009048226

Manufactured in the United States of America
1 – VI – 7/15/10

Contents

This cute cover-up will keep your clothes clean
while you work in the kitchen.

Kitchen Cover-up

Here is what you need:

white craft glue

trim

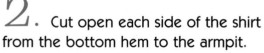

scissors

man's button-down
shirt with a pocket

Here is what you do:

1. Cut the collar and both arms off the shirt.

2. Cut open each side of the shirt from the bottom hem to the armpit.

4

3. Cut away both of the front panels of the shirt as shown. Leave enough fabric at the top to keep one button to close the apron.

4. If one of the discarded front panels has a pocket, cut around the pocket so that it keeps its backing.

5. Glue the pocket to the center of the back of the shirt. (The back of the shirt will be the front of the cover-up.)

6. Glue trim around the neck and the arm openings of the cover-up.

7. Use the trim to form the initial of the person who will be wearing the cover-up. Glue the initial to the pocket.

Use a woman's shirt if you are making the cover-up for a small child.

The clip on this recipe box displays a recipe for easy reading.

Recipe Box and Holder

Here is what you need:

box bottom a little more than 5 inches (13 cm) wide so that it can hold 3 x 5-inch (7.5 x 13-cm) index cards. It should be about 3 inches (7.5 cm) high and at least 3 inches (7.5 cm) deep.

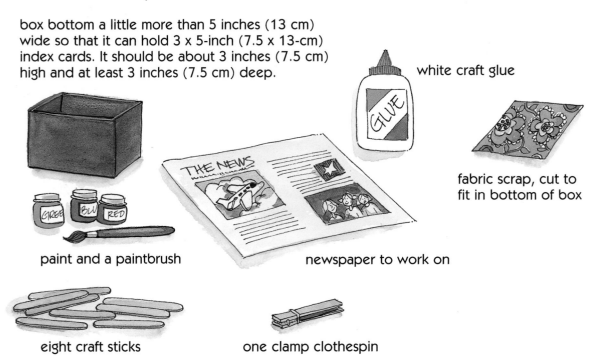

white craft glue

fabric scrap, cut to fit in bottom of box

paint and a paintbrush

newspaper to work on

eight craft sticks

one clamp clothespin

Here is what you do:

1. Glue a row of seven craft sticks down the wide part of the box, which will be the front, to form a decorative panel.

2. Glue the remaining craft stick to the center of the back of the box so that about half of the craft stick shows above the box's rim.

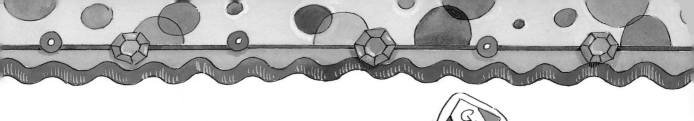

3. Glue the clamp clothespin, clamp end up, to the back of the top part of the stick. Position the clothespin so that about 1 inch (2.5 cm) of it sticks up above the top of the craft stick.

4. Paint the clothespin and the entire box, inside and out.

5. Once the box is dry, decorate the inside by gluing a piece of fabric into the bottom.

6. Make a small label to glue to the front of the box. You can print a label using the computer or write on a label by hand.

No more lost recipes or smudgy fingerprints! Put the recipe you are using into the clip, and it will always be in sight.

Keep track of recipes without removing them from your recipe box before they are needed.

Recipe Cards and Markers

Here is what you need:

large craft gems

white craft glue

scissors

blank 3 x 5-inch (7.5 x 13-cm) index cards

fancy-edge scissors

large colored paper clips

thin craft ribbon in lots of colors

Here is what you do:

1. Use fancy-edge scissors to cut a pattern along the right edge of each card. Glue ribbon on the right edge and top of each card.

2. Copy or paste your favorite recipes onto the cards.

3. Glue a craft gem to the upper portion of each paper clip. Keep the shorter side of the paper clip facing you as you glue.

4. Mark your recipe by slipping a jeweled paper clip over the top of the card.

You might want to color code your recipes by using a certain color gem for a certain type of recipe.

Add some glamour to cleaning up the kitchen!

Decorated Rubber Gloves

Here is what you need:

scissors

one pair
of rubber gloves

craft ribbon

permanent markers

Here is what you do:

1. Use the markers to add "nail polish" to the fingertips of the gloves.

2. Use the markers to add one or more rings and bracelets to the gloves.

3. Fold over the top cuff of the glove, and cut an even number of 1/4-inch (0.6 cm) slits around the cuff.

4. Weave craft ribbon in and out of the slits. Tie the two ends of the ribbon in a pretty bow on the topside of the glove.

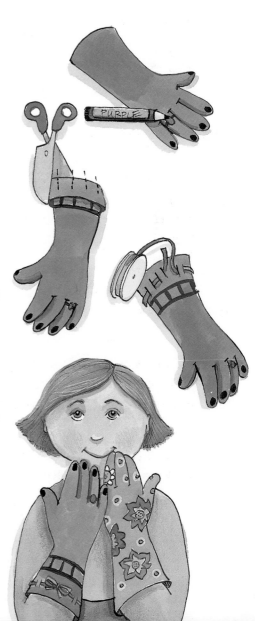

**Try using the markers to decorate
your gloves a different way.
How about covering them with red
hearts or flowers?**

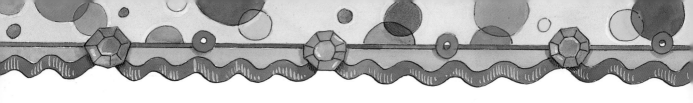

These cherries are kept on the outside of the refrigerator.

Cheery Cherry Photo Magnet

Here is what you need:

two pry-off bottle caps

craft magnet

green felt scrap

green embroidery floss

small photo

twist tie

scissors

red paint and a paintbrush

white craft glue

newspaper to work on

Here is what you do:

1. Working on the newspaper, paint the outside of both bottle caps red. They will be the front and the back of the cherry.

2. Cut a 2-inch (5 cm) piece of twist tie. Glue it into one of the bottle caps, leaving about half of it sticking out.

3. Cut a 2-inch (5 cm) piece of the green embroidery floss. Rub the floss with glue and twist it to secure all the fibers together. Press the gluey floss into the bottle cap alongside the twist tie, leaving about 3/4 of it sticking out beyond the cap. Let dry—the floss will stiffen to become the cherry stem.

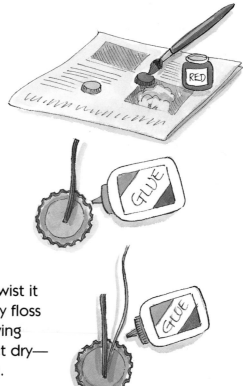

4. Cut a small photo to fit inside the cap. Glue it in place, so that the twist tie and stem align with the top of the photo subject's head.

5. Slide the other bottle cap over the loose end of the stem and under the loose end of the twist tie. With the two caps touching, glue the twist tie into the second bottle cap. Let dry.

6. Cut a circle of felt to glue inside the front cap of the cherry.

7. Flip down the top of the cherry. Cut two leaves for the cherry from the green felt. Glue the leaves together with the top of the stem between them.

8. Glue the craft magnet behind the leaves.

To view the photo inside the magnet, just open the front of the cherry.

11

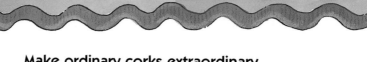

Make ordinary corks extraordinary.

Party Cork

Here is what you need:

ruler

cork

pony beads

paper clip

white craft glue

pipe cleaners and/or sparkle stems

scissors

Here is what you do:

1. Use an end of the paper clip to poke three holes in the top of the cork.

2. Cut three pieces of pipe cleaner or sparkle stem, 4 to 5 inches (10 to 13 cm) long.

3. Wrap each piece around your finger to make a spiral.

4. Thread a few colorful pony beads on each spiral. Secure the end by folding it over the last bead.

5. Dip the other end of each spiral in glue and stick in a hole in the top of the cork.

Make sets of corks in different color combinations for different holidays.

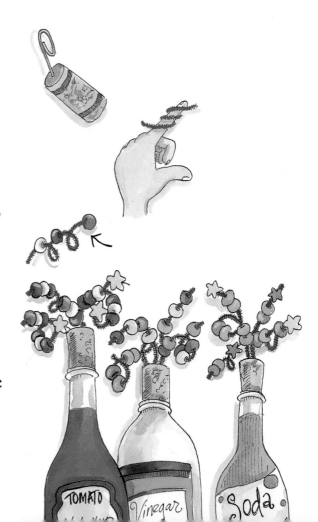

Start your party right with napkins that everyone will notice.

Pretty Paper Napkins

Here is what you need:

paper napkins in a
solid bright color

print fabric

scissors

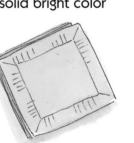

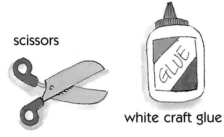

white craft glue

Here is what you do:

1. Cut a simple shape from the front corner of an open paper napkin. If you are making a symmetrical shape, folding the napkin and cutting through two layers will give you a nice, even design.

2. Glue a small square of fabric on the back of the napkin behind the shape so that the fabric shows through the opening. Use a very thin line of glue, or it will show through the napkin.

3. Glue a second, identical napkin behind the first napkin to cover the fabric back. Use a very thin layer of glue on the edges of the napkin to join them together.

Make a whole set of pretty paper napkins for your next party!

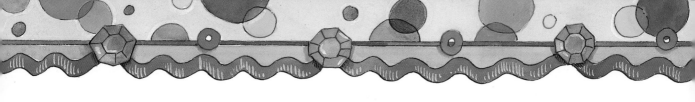

Beautiful napkins deserve a beautiful napkin holder.

Napkin Basket

Here is what you need:

white craft glue

package of paper napkins

scissors

two coordinating
pieces of print fabric

seam binding in a color that
looks nice with your fabric

ruler

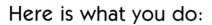

light cardboard at least 4
inches (10 cm) taller and
wider than your napkins

thin craft ribbon in a color that
looks nice with your fabric

pencil

small hole punch

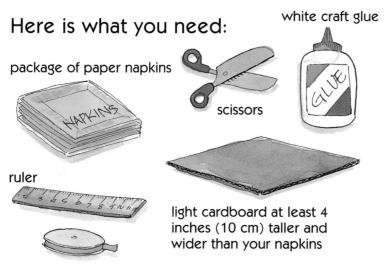

Here is what you do:

1. Set a folded napkin in the center
of the light cardboard, and trace around
the napkin with the pencil.

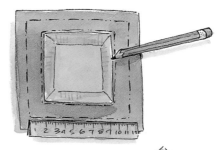

2. Draw another square around the
first square, making it about 2 inches
(5 cm) larger than the first square on all
four sides.

3. Cut out the large square.

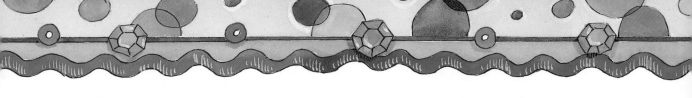

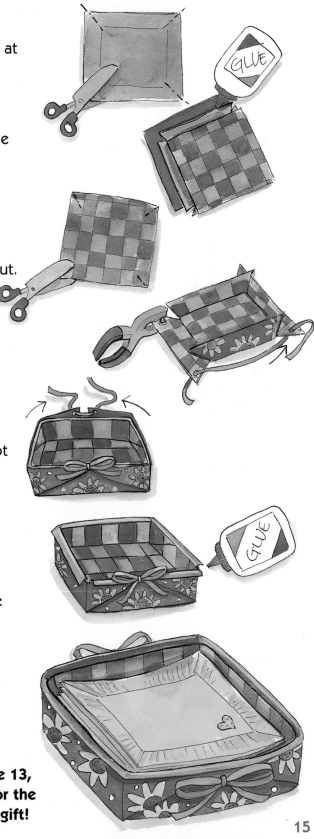

4. Cut from the corner of the large square to the edge of the traced napkin at each of the four corners.

5. Cut two squares of fabric the same size as the large square, and glue one onto each side.

6. Cut through the fabric at each corner where the cardboard has been cut.

7. Fold two opposite sides of the square up.

8. Punch a small hole in the end of each of the four points that you have not yet folded up.

9. Thread ribbon through the two holes of the points of the sides across from each other, and tie the ribbon in a bow so the side is secured. Do the same with the opposite side.

10. Glue folded seam binding around the top edge of the basket.

If you make the special napkins on page 13, you could use the same fabric pattern for the basket and the napkins. What a lovely gift!

15

It will be easy to take a quick peek into the slow cooker
with this knob cover in place.

Slow-Cooker Hat

Here is what you need:

two socks of
different colors

pom-pom

small rubber band

white craft glue

scissors

Here is what you do:

1. Cut the toe off each of the socks,
3 inches (7.5 cm) from the end.

2. Place the rubber band around the
opening of the toe of one sock.

3. Cover the sock piece and rubber band
with the second toe.

4. Roll the cut edges of both toe pieces over the rubber band to form a little hat with a rolled brim.

5. Secure the brim with small dots of glue. Do not run glue around the entire brim, or the brim will not stretch properly to fit over the knob of the slow-cooker lid.

6. Glue a pom-pom to the top of the sock hat.

The hat will help protect fingers from the heated knob on the lid of a slow-cooker.

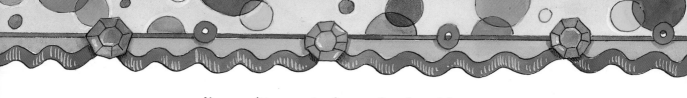

Keep critters out of your food and jazz up
your picnic table at the same time.

Decorated Bowl Covers

Here is what you need:

artificial flowers

permanent markers

disposable shower
caps, solid shade

paper fasteners

Here is what you do:

To make a flower-topped cover:

1. Separate the petals from two or
more artificial flowers by pulling out the
plastic centers.

2. Choose two or three layers of
petals that look well stacked together to
make a new flower.

3. Attach the flower to the
center of the plastic shower cap
using a paper fastener.

To make an art cover:

1. Use the markers to make your
own design on the outside of the
plastic shower cap.

**Can you think of other ways to
decorate the plastic covers?**

Did you ever think that your doll could help you with your table setting?

Napkin Doll

Here is what you need:

fabric scrap

colored, plastic-coated paper clips

thin craft ribbon

small paper napkins

11-inch (28 cm) doll with stand

Here is what you do:

1. If the doll does not have a dress, wrap the doll in fabric and tie a piece of ribbon in a bow around the waist to secure. If the doll already has a dress, just tie the ribbon around the waist of the dress.

2. Slide ten or more paper clips over the ribbon at the waist so they hang down.

3. Make a paper skirt for the doll by attaching the corner of a napkin to each paper clip. Spread the clips out evenly around the doll so that the napkins form a pretty skirt.

A larger doll can hold larger napkins.

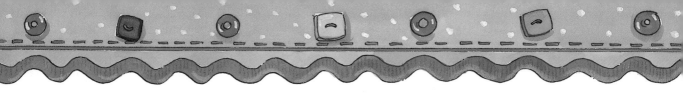

Don't toss out those old flip-flops!

Flip-Flops Trivet

Here is what you need:

pencil

white craft glue

scissors

pair of old flip-flops, washed, of course!

½-inch-wide (1.25 cm) decorative trim

heavy-duty aluminum foil

Here is what you do:

1. Cut the straps off both flip-flops.

2. Wrap both flip-flops with three layers of foil. Make sure the folds and seams are on the bottoms.

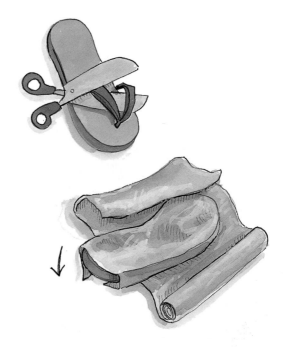

3. Find the holes in the flip-flops through which the straps were strung.

4. Use the pencil to poke the foil down into the holes so that the holes show.

5. Cut pieces of trim to go from the center hole to each side of the flip-flops so that they look like straps.

6. Push the ends of the trim into the holes and secure with glue.

7. Use the trivets separately, or if you want one larger trivet, glue the two flip-flops together side by side.

This project is perfect for summer cookouts!

Make a marker instead of making a mark in your cookbook.

Cookbook Page Markers

Here is what you need:

wood craft sticks, 2 for each
marker you wish to make

paint and a paintbrush

white craft glue

scissors

craft gems

newspaper to work on

Here is what you do for each marker:

1. Cut one craft stick in half with scissors. Trim away any rough edges. Do not worry about splits in the wood. The glue and paint will cover them and strengthen the wood.

2. Working on the newspaper, use the paint and paintbrush to paint the whole stick and the two halves of the cut stick. Paint one side first, let it dry, and then paint the other side.

3. Glue a half stick, round end up, to the front of the top quarter of the whole stick.

4. Glue the other half stick to the back of the whole stick so it is directly behind the front half stick.

5. Turn the stick so that the half sticks are on the bottom. Glue craft gems to the top portion of the whole stick.

To mark a favorite recipe, slip the double end of the marker over the cookbook page you will want to find again.

No more messy spoon prints on your counter!

Leaf Spoon Rest

Here is what you need:

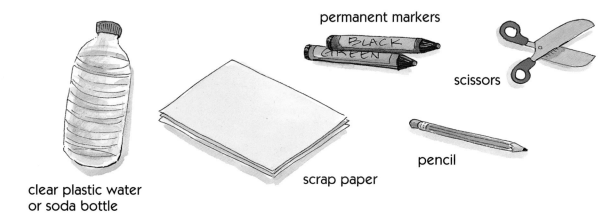

permanent markers

scissors

pencil

scrap paper

clear plastic water
or soda bottle

Here is what you do:

1. Use a leaf pattern outline if you have one. Otherwise, draw a 3- to 4-inch (7.5 to 10 cm) leaf on the scrap paper to use as a pattern. Cut the leaf pattern out.

2. Ask an adult to cut the bottom off of a plastic bottle to make it easier for you to cut into the side.

3. From the side of the plastic bottle, use scissors to cut a piece large enough to trace the leaf pattern on it.

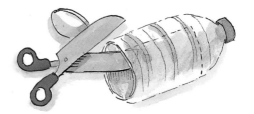

4. Use a black marker to trace the pattern on the rounded piece of plastic bottle with the stem of the leaf at the bottom.

5. Cut the leaf shape out of the plastic.

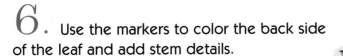

6. Use the markers to color the back side of the leaf and add stem details.

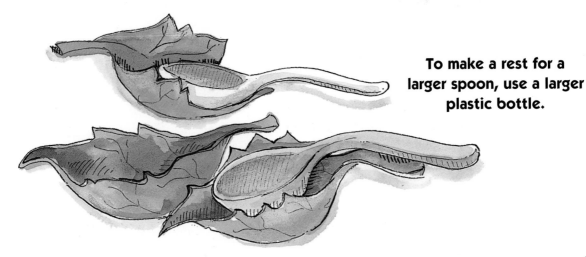

To make a rest for a larger spoon, use a larger plastic bottle.

Put these birds to work—they can hold a place card or a recipe or a sign telling the name of a special dish at a party buffet.

Bird Holders

Here is what you need:

yellow or orange felt

white craft glue

ruler

paint and a paintbrush

scissors

old pointed party hats

wiggle eyes

construction paper

Here is what you do for each bird:

1. Cut the tip off a pointed party hat 3 inches (7.5 cm) from the top.

2. Cut a ½-inch (1.25 cm) slit in the tip of the cut piece to slide a small card in.

3. If you like the pattern on the hat, leave it. Otherwise, paint the tip.

4. Cut two small triangles from the yellow or orange felt for the beak. Glue one triangle on each side of the slit at the point.

5. Glue two wiggle eyes below the beak.

6. Cut wings for the bird from felt.

7. Glue the wings to the back of the bird, below the eyes.

8. Cut small cards from construction paper to use as place cards or labels. Insert a card in the beak of each bird you are using.

A single bird is perfect for displaying a recipe card while cooking.

Fill this beautiful container with kitchen gadgets for a great gift.

Cooking Utensils Holder

Here is what you need:

tin can at least
7 inches (18 cm) tall

paint and a paintbrush

newspaper to work on

glass plant gems
or small rocks

scissors

seed beads

thin craft wire

white craft glue

plastic spoon

Here is what you do:

1. Working on newspaper, paint the outside of the can.

2. Cover the inside of the bottom of the can with glue, and cover with glass gems or pebbles. This will add weight to the bottom of the can to help keep it from tipping over.

3. Cut a 2-foot (61 cm) length of wire.

4. Wrap one end of the wire around the top part of the handle of the spoon. Thread seed beads on the wire as you wrap it around the handle. As you wrap the wire, arrange the beads so that they are all on the front of the handle.

5. When you are happy with the way the handle looks, tie off the wire and trim any excess.

6. Glue the decorated spoon to the can.

You might want to glue more than one decorated utensil on your can.

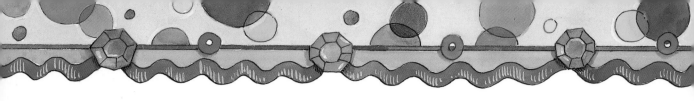

Paper plates can be even fancier than your nice china!

Party Plates

Here is what you need:

paper plates of the same size in two different colors

scissors

white craft glue

paper cups

thin craft ribbon

paper bowls

hole and shape punches

Here is what you do:

Punched Pattern Serving Plate

1. Punch a border of shapes around the edge of a plate.

2. Glue a plate of a different color behind the punched plate so that the color shows through the shapes.

3. To make into a serving plate, turn a paper bowl or cup over to make a stand for the plate. Glue the decorated plate to the bottom center of the inverted bowl or cup.

Ribbon Serving Plate

1. Punch an even number of plain holes around the edge of a plate.

2. Weave thin ribbon in and out of the holes. When the ends meet, tie them in a pretty bow.

3. Glue a second plate to the back to finish.

4. To make into a serving plate, turn a paper bowl or cup over to make a stand for the plate. Glue the decorated plate to the bottom center of the inverted bowl or cup.

How clever!

This is a book that you will read again and again!

Clipped Recipe Book

Here is what you need:

colored or printed paper

gallon-size zip-to-close plastic bags

self-stick address labels

scissors

permanent markers

hole punch

thin craft ribbon

white craft glue

discarded food magazines

Here is what you do:

1. Make a bag for each recipe category—desserts, main dishes, vegetables, etc. You can easily add more bags to the book later.

2. Line each bag with colored or printed paper.

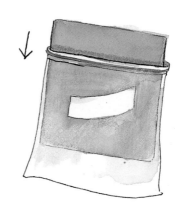

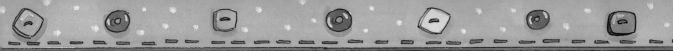

3. Use a permanent marker to write the name of the category of recipe to be stored in the bag on the white space provided on the bag. If there is no white space, then add a self-stick label and write the category on it.

4. Punch a hole in the top left corner of each bag you make.

5. Cut pictures of food from each of your categories from food magazines, and use the pictures to decorate your bags. Glue won't stick directly to the plastic bags, so you can glue your food pictures to a piece of colored paper and slip it into the bag.

6. Tie the bags together loosely with a piece of thin craft ribbon tied in a bow.

Store clipped recipes in the zip-to-close pages of the book.

Swat those pesky flies away in style!

Fancy Flyswatter

Here is what you need:

yellow pipe cleaner

new flyswatter

scissors

artificial flowers

Here is what you do:

1. Pull the plastic centers out of two or more artificial flowers. Separate the petals.

2. Choose two or more different colored petals to stack together to make a new flower.

3. Cut a 3-inch (7.5 cm) piece of the yellow pipe cleaner.

4. Fold the piece of pipe cleaner in half. Thread the two ends up through the top corner of the mesh swatter.

5. Thread the ends through the hole in the center of the stack of flower petals.

6. Fold the ends of the pipe cleaner in half and to opposite sides to secure the flower to the swatter.

7. Make a second flower in the same way, and secure it to the handle.

A very unusual gift!

35

Coupons only work for you when you can find them easily.

Coupon Holder

Here is what you need:

paint and a paintbrush

white craft glue

newspaper to work on

colored paper

pasta box with a window, such as a macaroni box

variety of ribbons and trims

scissors

hole punch

markers

Here is what you do:

1. Cut away the top one-third of the front and sides of the box.

2. Round off the corners of the back of the box.

3. Punch a hole in the center of the back top of the box so it can be hung.

4. If the box has a cellophane window on the front, remove the cellophane.

5. Working on newspaper, paint the entire box, inside and out.

6. Cut a piece of the colored paper to glue on the bottom of the box.

7. Cut a rectangle of colored paper to glue behind the open window on the front of the box. If there is no window, just glue the rectangle to the front of the box.

8. Use the markers to write the name of the person the box is for and "coupons" on the paper.

9. Glue trims and ribbons around the front and sides of the box to decorate it.

Very handy!

Here's a great idea to help you keep those plastic bags for reuse.

Scrubbie Bag Dispenser

Here is what you need:

ruler

bath scrubbie

pony beads

variety of colorful ribbons

scissors

Here is what you do:

1. Cut the center rope of the bath scrubbie. Then open the mesh so that you have a long tube.

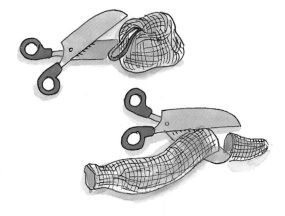

2. Cut a 2-foot (61 cm) piece from the tube to use for the bag dispenser.

3. Close one end of the tube by tying a piece of ribbon around it.

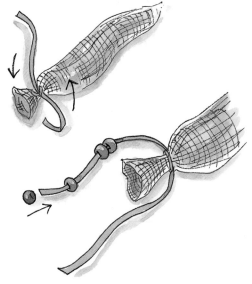

4. Thread some pony beads on the ribbon, tying them in place if necessary.

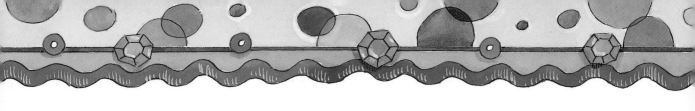

5. Tie the two ends of the ribbon together to make a hanger for the dispenser.

6. Tie lots of long pieces of pretty ribbon around the top of the bag dispenser so that the ends hang down around the bag.

7. Thread pony beads on some or all the ribbons, and glue the beads in place.

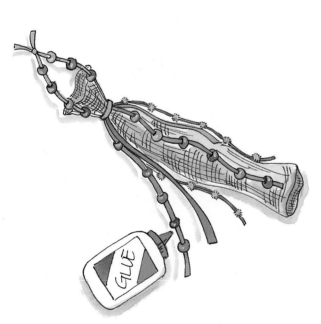

You don't need to tie off the open end of the tube. The stretchy mesh will hold any bags that are stuffed inside it and will easily release them as they are needed.

Kitchen notes are important—especially phone messages.

Kitchen Scratch Pads

Here is what you need:

scissors

pencil

white copy paper

white craft glue

discarded magazines with food, appliance, and tabletop pictures

stapler

colored paper

Here is what you do:

1. Look through the magazines to find a kitchen-related picture for the cover of the scratch pad. Pictures from magazine covers work especially well because they are heavy and shiny.

2. Cut the picture out.

3. Fold a sheet of colored paper in half.

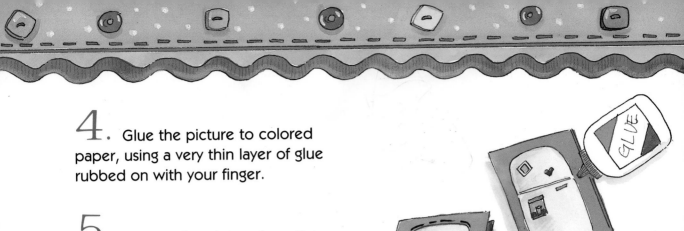

4. Glue the picture to colored paper, using a very thin layer of glue rubbed on with your finger.

5. Cut out the picture from the folded paper so you have a shape to use as the back cover of the pad.

6. Trace the cover shape on the white paper.

7. Cut fourteen shapes from the white paper for the inside of the scratch pad.

8. Stack the papers with the picture on the front and the colored paper shape at the back of the stack.

9. Staple the pages together.

Make a set of several scratch pads to give as a gift.

This holder will keep your string untangled and ready to use.

String and Scissors Holder

Here is what you need:

square tissue box

large pom-pom

decorative yarn

paint and a paintbrush

newspaper to work on

cardboard toilet paper tube

scissors

white craft glue

craft foam

hole punch

Here is what you do:

1. Cut the top of the tissue box on three sides so that it will open and close.

2. Remove the cellophane from behind the opening on the top of the tissue box.

3. Glue the large pom-pom inside one end of the cardboard tube to close it.

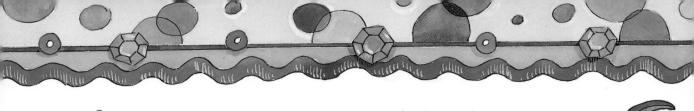

4. Working on newspaper, paint the entire tissue box and cardboard tube inside and out. Let dry.

5. Punch a hole in the center edge of the lid on the side that is opposite the hinge. Punch a second hole in the side of the box below the first hole.

6. Thread a 12-inch (30 cm) piece of decorative yarn through the two holes. Tie the yarn in a bow to secure the lid closed.

7. Glue yarn around the box to make a decorative band. Glue yarn around the oval opening at the top of the box.

8. Glue a square of craft foam to the bottom of the box.

9. Glue the tube to the back of the box with the open end at the top.

Untie the lid to place a ball of string in the box with the end hanging out from the oval opening. Tie the lid shut to keep the ball of string in place. Put a pair of scissors in the tube at the back of the box.

43

Here is a great idea for marking stemmed glasses at a fancy party.

Glass Collars

Here is what you need:

old greeting cards

white craft glue

scissors

pen

3-inch (7.5 cm) diameter glass or paper cup to use as a pattern

collage materials

Here is what you do:

1. Find a section of the greeting card that will make a nice circular picture or pattern.

2. Use the pen to trace around the glass or cup pattern on that area of the card.

3. Cut out the circle.

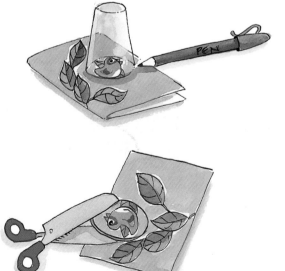

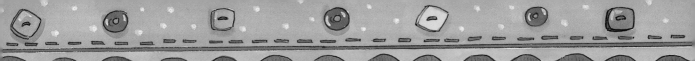

4. Cut from the edge to the center of the circle.

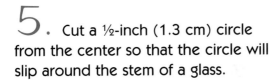

5. Cut a ½-inch (1.3 cm) circle from the center so that the circle will slip around the stem of a glass.

6. If you want to decorate a plain circle, make glass collars from the blank backs of greeting cards. Collage materials such as craft gems, sequins, and stickers make lovely, unique decorations.

7. You might want to leave a space on the collar to write the name of the person using the glass.

Make glass collars for holiday parties by using greeting cards from the holiday being celebrated.

Protect your surfaces and show off your crafting ability at the same time.

Clever Coasters

Here is what you need:

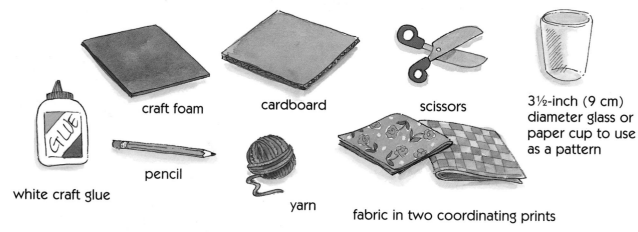

white craft glue

GLUE

craft foam

cardboard

scissors

3½-inch (9 cm) diameter glass or paper cup to use as a pattern

pencil

yarn

fabric in two coordinating prints

Here is what you do:

1. Use the pencil to make a 3½-inch (9 cm) circle on the cardboard. A drinking glass would make a good circle to trace around. Cut out the circle to use as a pattern.

2. Use the pattern to trace one circle from the craft foam for each coaster you are making. Cut out the circle.

3. Use the pattern to trace two fabric circles, one from each print fabric, for each coaster you are making. Cut out the circles.

4. Glue one fabric circle, print side out, on each side of a foam circle. Use a different pattern for the top and bottom of each coaster.

5. Rub glue around the outer edge of each coaster, and cover the edge with yarn.

You can make the coasters all alike or in a variety of different prints and colors.

About the Author

Kathy Ross is the author of more than fifty books with more than one million copies in print. Her name has become synonymous with "top quality craft books." Following twenty-five years of developing nursery school programs and guiding young children through craft projects, Ross has authored many successful series, including Crafts for Kids Who Are Learning about . . ., Girl Crafts, and All New Holiday Crafts for Kids.